PIANO / VOCAL / GUITAR

SPECTACULAR!™

MUSIC FROM THE NICKELODEON ORIGINAL MOVIE

ISBN 978-1-4234-8113-3

HAL•LEONARD® CORPORATION
7777 W BLUEMOUND RD P O BOX 13819 MILWAUKEE WI 53213

In Australia Contact:
Hal Leonard Australia Pty. Ltd.
4 Lentara Court
Cheltenham, Victoria, 3192 Australia
Email: ausadmin@halleonard.com.au

Visit Hal Leonard Online at
www.halleonard.com

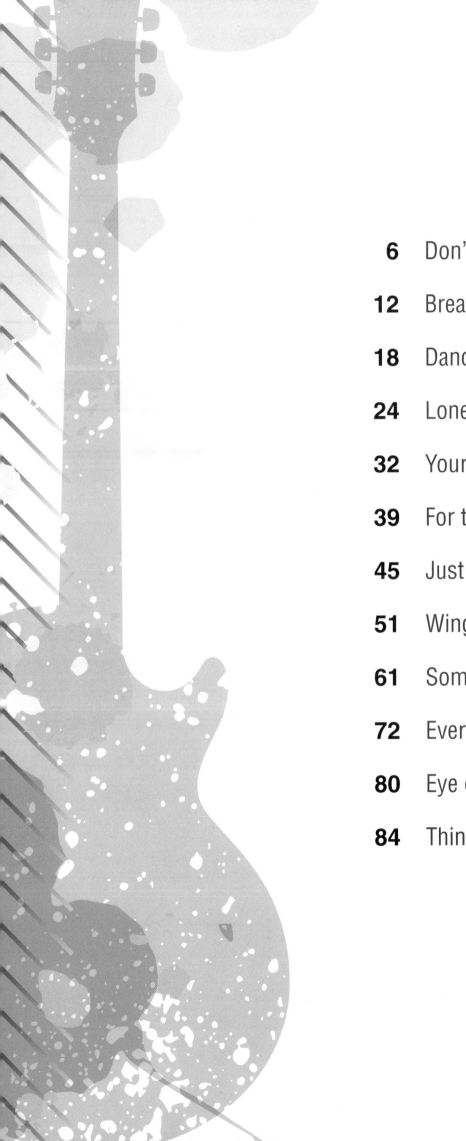

6 Don't Tell Me

12 Break My Heart

18 Dance with Me

24 Lonely Love Song

32 Your Own Way

39 For the First Time

45 Just Freak

51 Wings of a Dream

61 Something to Believe In

72 Everything Can Change

80 Eye of the Tiger

84 Things We Do for Love

DON'T TELL ME

Words and Music by MATTHEW GERRARD
and ROBBIE NEVIL

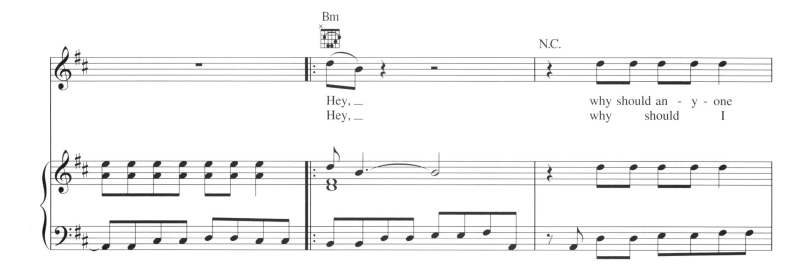

They can say what they like; _

I don't hear it at all. _____

It's _ my _ life _ to live; _ I live _____ it just the way I want. _

_____ I'm nev - er hold - ing back. _____ I

BREAK MY HEART

Words and Music by MATTHEW GERRARD
and ROBBIE NEVIL

Lyrics:

So you're the girl; I heard the ru- mor.
Stare me down; in- tim- i- date me.
You got the boys
Ba- by, please;

wrapped a- round your fin- ger.
you'll nev- er break me.
Such a sweet
Bring it on,

Recorded a half step higher.

Yeah.

DANCE WITH ME

Words and Music by MATTHEW GERRARD
and ROBBIE NEVIL

Dance beat

Try to o-ver-think a sim-ple
Talk-in' 'bout as-trol-o-gy is

sit-u-a-tion,   you can miss your   chance; ___   'cause
fas-ci-nat-ing;   I'd rath-er groove with   you. ___

I'm not real-ly look-ing for a con-ver-sa-tion,
How long are you real-ly gon-na keep me wait-ing? Tell me,

LONELY LOVE SONG

Words and Music by MATTHEW GERRARD
and ROBBIE NEVIL

Moderately fast

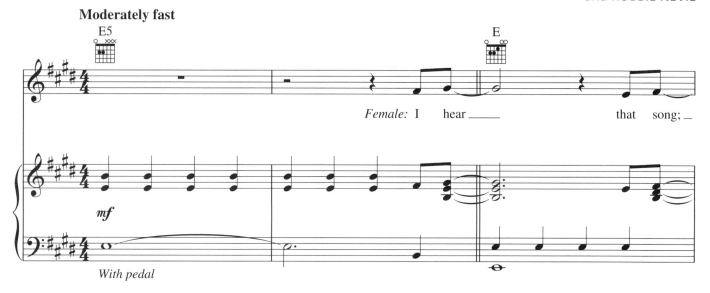

Female: I hear ____ that song; ____

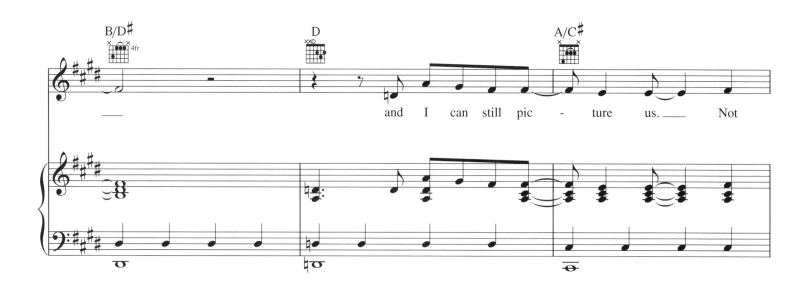

____ and I can still pic - ture us. ____ Not

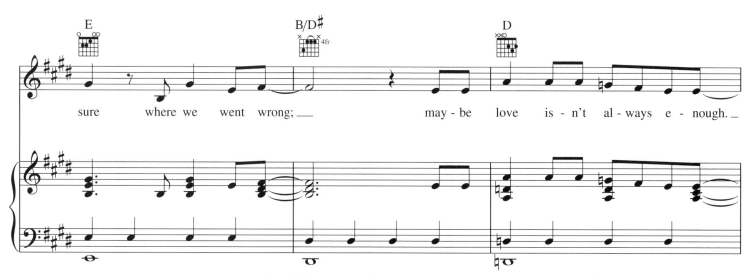

sure where we went wrong; ____ may - be love is - n't al - ways e - nough. ____

YOUR OWN WAY

Words and Music by MATTHEW GERRARD
and ROBBIE NEVIL

FOR THE FIRST TIME

Words and Music by MATTHEW GERRARD
and ROBBIE NEVIL

Recorded a half step lower.

JUST FREAK

Words and Music by MATTHEW GERRARD
and ROBBIE NEVIL

Ah, ___ ah, ___ ah.

When the mu- sic takes you, don't stop.
Got- ta work it; turn it on, now.

WINGS OF A DREAM

Words and Music by MATTHEW GERRARD,
ROBBIE NEVIL and JAY LANDERS

* Recorded a whole step higher.

SOMETHING TO BELIEVE IN

Words and Music by MATTHEW GERRARD
and ROBBIE NEVIL

Male: I used to see the world as cold, so cold.

Female: I always felt so all alone, oh.

EVERYTHING CAN CHANGE

Words and Music by MATTHEW GERRARD
and ROBBIE NEVIL

Recorded a half step higher.

EYE OF THE TIGER

Words and Music by FRANK SULLIVAN
and JIM PETERIK

So man-y times _____ it hap-pens too fast. _____
Face to face, _____ out in the heat, _____
Ris - in' up, _____ straight to the top. _____

You trade your pas - sion for glo - ry.
hang - in' tough, stay - in' hun - gry.
Had the guts, got the glo - ry.

Don't lose your grip _____ on the
They stack the odds, _____ still we
Went the dis - tance. Now I'm

dreams of the past. You must fight just to keep them a - live. _____
take to the street for the kill with the skill to sur - vive. _____
not gon - na stop, just a girl and her will to sur - vive. _____

THE THINGS WE DO FOR LOVE

Words and Music by GRAHAM GOULDMAN
and ERIC STEWART

Recorded a half step lower.